HYPER HOLY HAPPENINGS

Andy Robb

Hyper Holy Happenings

Copyright © 2001 John Hunt Publishing Ltd
Text © 2001 Andy Robb
Illustrations © 2001 Andy Robb.
Reprinted 2003

ISBN 1-84298- 047-5

Design by Nautilus Design, UK

Scriptures quoted from the Good News Bible published by The Bible
Societies/HarperCollins Publishers Ltd., UK,
© American Bible Society,1966, 1971, 1976, 1992.

Write to:
John Hunt Publishing Ltd
46A West Street
Alresford
Hampshire
SO24 9AU
UK

The rights of Andy Robb as author and illustrator of this work have been
asserted in accordance with the Copyright, Designs and Patents Act 1988.

A CIP catalogue record for this book is available from the British Library.

Printed by Tien Wah Press Ltd. Singapore

CONTENTS

Introduction

What's the most boring
thing you can think of?
Okay, now multiply it by
a zillion.
That's how boring a lot of
people think the Bible is.
The funny thing is, most
people who think the
Bible's mega mind-
numbingly boring have
never even read it!
Crazy or what?!

Imagine turning down a triple whopper chicken, cheese and
yoghurt burger with gherkin and custard relish just because
you'd never tried it...

On second thoughts that wasn't such a good suggestion.
But you get my point?
I mean, I'll bet you didn't even know that the Bible's got adverts
in it to tell people what's going to happen in the future or that
it told people that the world was round thousands of years
before we'd worked it out.
There's so much stuff in the Bible we won't be able to look at
every bit of it but the bits we've chosen will hopefully make you
start to realise that the Bible maybe isn't quite so boring as you
thought.
Have fun!

So What's The Bible All About?

The Bible isn't just one whopping great book.
It's actually 66 not-quite-so-whopping books all whacked
together like a sort of mini library.

The first book in the Bible is called Genesis, which was also the name of a pop group your parents once liked but they won't admit to it even if you hang them from the ceiling by their toenails... and the last book is called Revelation which as far as I know wasn't the name of a pop group your parents once liked.

To keep things simple, the Bible is mainly about two things.

God.
And people.

Who wrote the Bible?
People.

Who decided what to write about?
God.

So how did they know what God wanted them to write?
Did God send an e-mail?

Not quite.
Here's one way of looking at it.
Imagine two people in love.

Enough of that!
Sorry, have I put you off your lunch?
When people are in love with each other all they want to do is
spend every waking hour gazing lovingly into each other's eyes.
(I know, it's horrible, isn't it!)

The way they hug and cuddle each other you wonder whether they've been permanently super-glued to each other for all eternity.

It even gets to the point where they start to think each other's thoughts.

Well, that's sort of what it was like for the guys who wrote the Bible (without the cuddling bit).

They spent so much time with God that they got to know what he was thinking and what he wanted to say.

Sometimes God even spoke to them in dreams or gave them visions of what he wanted to say.

They were totally in touch with God so that what they wrote was as if God had written it himself.

So what sort of things does God want to say to us?

For starters, the Bible tells us that there is a God and that he made you and me and the whole universe.

It also tells us that he wants us to be his friends and how we can do that.

What good is a book that was written *even before* my mum and dad were born? People might not wear silly costumes like they did in the past but God hasn't changed a bit so what he had to say to people with funny headdresses and sandals thousands of years ago is still important for us.

This Boring Bible book's all about what happened after Jesus died, came back to life and then went to heaven. Most of the action is taken from a book in the New Testament bit of the Bible called **Acts** but there are also lots of letters and other stuff as well.

(By the way, I was only joking about hanging your parents upside down by their toenails - nose hairs work much better!!!)

Do you play in a football team?

Imagine that you've just had your most successful season, *ever*, and it's all down to the fact that you've got the world's best manager.

There you are dreaming of even greater success next season when, horror of horrors, your manager suddenly clears off.

How would you feel about that?

In the last Boring Bible book, *Super Son*, we found out all about Jesus (God's Son), who came down to earth to get rid of all the bad stuff in our lives that stops us being friends with God.

With his band of twelve disciples, Jesus criss-crossed the land of Israel healing people and telling them how God expected them to live.

Then, to finish off the job he'd been sent to do, Jesus allowed himself to be executed on a wooden cross.

(To find out *why*, you're going to have to read *Super Son* - that's if you haven't done it already!)

Amazingly, the Bible says that three days later, Jesus was brought back to life by God and for 40 days he showed himself to loads and loads of people (about *500* people if

you're picky about exact numbers), including the disciples.
I'll bet the disciples were half hoping that Jesus would stick
around for a bit so that they could have *another* successful
season with him.

All those healings and miracles.

All those crowds hanging on to Jesus's every word.

It was brilliant!

But, that wasn't God's plan.

Instead, Jesus went back up to heaven and the disciples were
left all alone.

Everyone say "Aah!".

Don't feel *too* sorry for them!
Just before Jesus left, he gave them a very important message...

That's because Jesus told them face to face.
It was just about the last thing he ever said to them...

So, that's exactly what the disciples did.
They hung around in Jerusalem and waited.

Not *that* kind of waiting!
Hanging around sort of waiting.

I wonder what was going through their minds?

What did Jesus mean by being baptised in the Holy Spirit?

They'd seen John the Baptist baptising people in the River
Jordan, plunging them under the water and back up again to
represent all the bad things in their lives being washed away.

But how could you get baptised by
the Holy Spirit?
Would the Holy Spirit make them
wet?
Perhaps they should go down by
the *river* and wait?
To be honest, I'll bet they didn't
know *what* to expect!
And how *long* were they going to
have to wait?

Fifty days after Jesus had been executed, their waiting came to a very abrupt end.

It was the Jewish festival of Pentecost and the disciples, along with heaps of other followers of Jesus, were crammed together in a house somewhere in Jerusalem (no doubt praying and worshipping God).

Suddenly, the place was filled with a loud noise.

It sounded like the rushing wind.

Without further warning, something that looked like tongues of fire spread out and touched everyone.

At last!
This was what they'd been waiting for.
God was baptising them with his Holy Spirit.
But this wasn't anything like being drenched with water.
They were being soaked with the Holy Spirit on the *inside*.

If you think that *this* was awesome then get yourself ready for what happened *next*!
Being filled with the Holy Spirit was such a brilliant thing that they couldn't contain themselves.
Everyone started to praise God and tell of all the wonderful things he had done, but not in their own language.
They found themselves speaking in lots of *different* languages.
In fact, they were speaking the languages of all the different nations that had come to Jerusalem to celebrate Pentecost.
When foreigners passing by heard their native languages being spoken they were dumbfounded.

Hang on a minute, it looks like one of the disciples is going to say something to the crowd.

Hey, isn't that Peter?

Wasn't he the cowardly one who pretended he didn't know Jesus when he was arrested?

Yep, that's him!

FELLOW JEWS AND ALL YOU WHO LIVE IN JERUSALEM. THESE PEOPLE AREN'T DRUNK... IT'S ONLY NINE O'CLOCK IN THE MORNING! IT'S WHAT THE PROPHET JOEL TALKED ABOUT YEARS AGO WHEN HE SAID THAT GOD WOULD POUR OUT HIS SPIRIT ON **EVERYONE!**

With the Holy Spirit living inside of him, Peter was now completely fearless.

Now he didn't mind *who* knew that he was a follower of Jesus. The Bible tells us that Peter went on to give everyone a no-messing lecture about Jesus so they'd know for sure *who* it was that had sent the Holy Spirit.

Okay, time to get your guessing brains on.

How many people do you think became followers of Jesus as a result of Peter's speech?

Draw a circle round the right answer.

Not bad for a morning's work.
And with 3000 new followers of Jesus, the first church was begun.

What do you imagine the first church looked like?

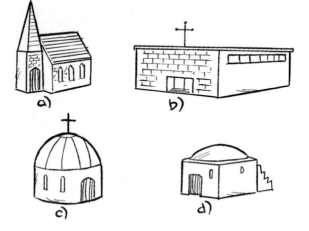

Just in case you were in any doubt, it was **d)**. (It's meant to be a picture of someone's house.)
A church in those days wasn't anything to do with the building. It was simply a group of people who followed Jesus, meeting together.

Not *all* of the 3000 new believers in Jesus would have stayed put in Jerusalem. Don't forget that some of them were just *visiting* for the Pentecost celebrations.

Here are some of the places the Bible tells us they came from.

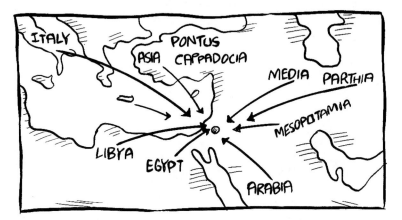

Once they got back home they'd be starting churches of their very own.

In such a short space of time the news about Jesus was already beginning to spread.

Before we move on, just in case you haven't got the foggiest idea who or what the Holy Spirit is, we're going to do a spot of detective work to find out.

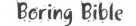

The Holy Spirit
INVESTIGATED!

What does the Bible tell us about the Holy Spirit?
Fact 1: The Holy Spirit is God.

A good question.
What *does* zis, I mean this, mean?
The Bible says that although there is just one God he's actually got *three* personalities.
(Yes, I know it sounds complicated but try not to think too hard about it - I'm not taking the blame for your brain exploding!)

Anyway, first off you've got God the **Father**.
(When you mention God to most people *he's* the one they usually imagine.)

Next we've got **Jesus**, God's Son - star of Boring Bible book *Super Son*.
(Jesus was the one who visited earth to get rid of our sin.)

And last but by no means least, there's the **Holy Spirit**.
So, in a nutshell, they're all God *together*...but they all do *different* jobs. Got it? Good!

Fact 2: The Holy Spirit was involved with creating the earth.
When God commanded the world to be made (check out Boring Bible book *Ballistic Beginnings*), it was the Holy Spirit who did all the work.

Fact 3: When God made the world's first man, Adam, he made him out of dirt and then breathed life into him.
Guess who the life was?
Yep, it was the Holy Spirit!

Fact 4: In the Old Testament bit of the Bible there are lots of stories about people God chose to do special jobs or to say things that God wanted them to say.
Who gave them the power or the words to do it?
No prizes here! Once again it was...the Holy Spirit.

Fact 5: When God decided to send Jesus to earth (from heaven), it was none other than the Holy Spirit who made Mary pregnant (full story in Boring Bible book *Super Son*).

YOU WOULD THEENK ZAT ZEE 'OLY SPEEREET WOULD BE, 'OW YOU SAY, EXHAUSTED, WIZ ALL ZAT 'ARD WORK.

Fact 6: God never gets tired out!

UNLIKE **ME**! ZIS CASE IS MAKING ME, 'OW YOU SAY, WHACKED!

Now we've got that all cleared up let's go and see what the
Holy Spirit's *next* mission was?

Your Next Mission....

...Jesus is back in heaven after sorting
out that nasty sin problem ...we've left
the disciples in charge of telling
people that they can now be friends with
God...but they will need the same power
that Jesus had inside him if they are
going to be effective...they need God's
power to help them ...this is a job
for you, Holy Spirit...

And I hope *you* do too.
Now, let's get back to the story...

If you've ever been to the theatre to see a play, the chances are it was split up into different acts. There's usually an interval in the middle to separate the acts.

(That's the time everyone races out to the foyer to join the queue for ice creams.)

Well, **'Acts'** is *also* the name of the book in the Bible that tells you about most of the action that happened soon after Jesus had gone back up to heaven and as the Holy Spirit started to kick-start the first lot of churches into life.

Boring Bible Fact: The book of Acts (which is quite a whopper with 28 chapters!) was written by a doctor called Luke. Acts was like Luke's follow-up book because he'd already written a book about Jesus's life.

Unsurprisingly, it's called 'Luke'. Luke didn't just write about some of the stuff that happened in the Bible he also appears in it as well, as one of a crowd of people who travelled around telling people about Jesus.
Acts was probably written around 60 AD-ish!

One afternoon, so the book of Acts tells us, Peter and John went off to the Temple to pray.

On their way in they were stopped by a lame beggar.

(The Temple was a good place to beg because the Jews were supposed to give money to beggars and poor people as part of their religion.)

If the beggar was expecting rich pickings from these two he had another think coming.

Taking the man by his right hand, Peter helped him to his feet. The man was completely healed!

To prove it, he started leaping and prancing around with joy.

In no time at all the Temple area was buzzing with the news of this miracle.

Not one to waste an opportunity, Peter started to tell the crowds about Jesus and how it was *his* power that had healed the cripple.

You'd think everyone would be thrilled with what had happened. No way!

If you *really* wanted to annoy the religious leaders then the quickest way was to start talking about Jesus.

They thought they'd heard the last of him when they had him executed a couple of months back and now here were Jesus's followers up to their old tricks again.

Peter and John were swiftly arrested by the Temple guards before they could do any more damage.

Next day they were brought before the religious top brass to explain their actions.

If you'd asked Peter that question a couple of months back he'd have tried to squirm his way out of an answer...

Now, filled with the Holy Spirit, he was full of courage...

The religious leaders were gobsmacked.
The couldn't get over the way an uneducated man like Peter
could speak so well.

How frustrating for them!

What were they to do?

They finally settled on warning Peter and John not to blab any more about Jesus.

Unfortunately for the religious leaders it was too late.

The whole of Jerusalem was already talking about the miraculous healing.

When Peter and John got back to the other believers everyone was over the moon with what God was doing.

They just couldn't seem to stop themselves from praising God.

But all was not sweetness and light amongst the believers...

JEWS NEWS

2 BELIEVERS DEAD!

Followers of the recently executed religious leader, Jesus of Nazareth, were shocked when two of their number were killed stone dead by God. Reports suggest that Ananias and his wife Sapphira had sold some of their property (in keeping with the practice of these believers of Jesus), to share the proceeds with less well off believers. But, in a secret pact, the pair had agreed to keep back some money for themselves. When confronted with their scheming, both Ananias and Sapphira lied about what they had done. Within hours of each other, they were both dead, struck down for lying to the Holy Spirit. News is reaching us, even as we go to print, that terror is sweeping the church. It would appear that being a follower of Jesus is a far more serious business than many at first thought.

INSIDE :- WIN A DAY OUT AT THE TEMPLE FOR ALL THE FAMILY!

With the Holy Spirit working through them, Peter and the other leaders of the believers (the Bible calls them 'apostles') performed more and more amazing miracles.

People were being healed left right and centre...some of them just by falling under Peter's shadow!

Now, I'll bet *you* don't suffer from jealousy, do you?

The Boring Bible Jealousy Test

	No Probs	Bit Miffed	Jealous	Maddeningly Jealous
1 You and your best mate audition for the same part in the school play...and *he* gets it! How do you feel?	☐	☐	☐	☐
2 Your brother/sister gets more Christmas presents than you! How do you feel?	☐	☐	☐	☐
3 Everyone in your class seems	☐	☐	☐	☐

3 Everyone in your class seems to be going somewhere exciting for their summer hols but you're only going away for a week in an old, leaky caravan! How do you feel?

4 The most popular kids at
your school always seem to
be the best looking or the best
at sport!
How do you feel?

No Probs ☐ Bit Miffed ☐ Jealous ☐ Maddeningly Jealous ☐

If all of your answers were 'Maddeningly Jealous' then you and
the religious leaders in our story have got a lot in common.
How they *hated* it when the apostles attracted the crowds.
Time to arrest them again!
Into jail went the apostles...but not for long.
The religious leaders hadn't banked on *God* being on the case.
At the dead of night, an angel from God came along and
opened up the prison gates and set them free again with these
words...

GO AND STAND IN THE
TEMPLE AND TELL PEOPLE
ALL ABOUT THIS
NEW LIFE!

When they found out they'd been outsmarted, the religious leaders had the apostles hauled back before them yet again. These followers of Jesus were beginning to cause them even *more* trouble than Jesus.

At least there was just *one* of him.

If they had their way, the apostles would go the same way as Jesus and be killed.

One of the religious leaders, Gamaliel, wasn't such a hot-head as the rest of them and suggested that if God *really was* with the apostles then fighting against them would be a complete waste of time.

On the other hand, if God *wasn't* with them then all the fuss would soon die down.

The other religious leaders grudgingly agreed to go along with Gamaliel but they didn't let the apostles get off scot-free.

They still had them whipped first and *then* released.

(There's justice for you!)

To be fair to the Jewish religious leaders, they weren't *all* bad. The Bible says that a great number of them actually became followers of Jesus.

The First Martyr

One of the believers in Jesus, called Stephen, really annoyed some of the Jews. Not only did he do amazing miracles but he also spoke with such wisdom that there was absolutely no arguing with him. That *really* got under their skin!

Some men were bribed to say that Stephen had said things against the Jewish religion...which he hadn't.

Stephen was tried before the Jewish Council and found guilty. The punishment they chose was stoning.

It was a horrible method of execution but it meant that they'd have the chance to kill Stephen personally and vent some of their anger and hatred.

The Bible says that as the Council fixed their eyes on Stephen it looked like he had the face of an angel.

Even as he gave up his last breath Stephen couldn't be faulted...

...and Stephen was dead.

He was the first follower of Jesus to be killed for what he believed (that's what a martyr is)...but definitely not the last!

Many years ago I was on holiday in the South of France. It was blisteringly hot and all over the hillsides, fires raged while aeroplanes circled above dropping cargoes of water in a desperate attempt to quench the blazing forest fires.

Most of these fires were probably started by just a small spark that then ignited the tinder-dry landscape into a blazing inferno.

The death of Stephen was the spark that started the cruel persecution of the followers of Jesus.

Such was the hatred that many Jews felt towards these believers of Jesus that they would go to *any* length to track them down and arrest them and even kill them.

As the believers scattered across the region they took with them the good news about Jesus.

Instead of killing off the church, persecution was making it grow!

Boring Bible Fact: The story of Jesus is called the 'gospel' which means 'good news' because that's exactly what it is!

The good news about Jesus soon reached Samaria, which had been a long-time enemy of the Jews.

THE DAILY SAMARITAN

MAN MISSING

A man who had only seconds before been baptising an official of the Queen of Ethopia, disappeared off the face of the earth. Philip, a follower of the much talked about, Jesus of Nazareth, had run alongside the official's chariot as it was

THE SCENE RIGHT AFTER PHILIP DISAPPEARED.

travelling along the road from Jerusalem to Gaza and explained the meaning of some Jewish scriptures that were puzzling him. On realising that they were about Jesus, the official, then and there, also became a believer in Jesus. Unconfirmed reports suggest that this Philip did, in fact, reappear in Azotus where he continued to speak out about Jesus.

INSIDE: YOUR CHANCE TO NOMINATE SOMEONE IN OUR FABULOUS
GOOD SAMARITAN OF THE YEAR
COMPETITION

If you've read Boring Bible book *Catastrophic Kings* then you'll remember a king by the name of Saul.
Well, we've now got *another* Saul coming onto the scene. *This* Saul started out nasty...

...but ended up nice.

Boring Bible Fact: When Stephen was getting stoned to death, Saul was the person who looked after everyone's cloaks.

We're going to need to keep our eye on Saul because something out of the ordinary is about to happen to him.
But first...

ALL ABOUT SAUL...

PLACE OF BIRTH: Tarsus in Cilicia, (which makes him a Roman citizen)

RELIGION: Jewish

SECT: Pharisee

TRIBE: Benjamin

EDUCATION: Taught by the great Gamaliel in Jerusalem

So, all in all, Saul was well and truly qualified to be an enemy of Jesus and his followers.

Saul had made it his business to persecute (that means to be against) the believers.
He went from house to house, dragging them out and throwing them in jail.

Saul wasn't content with just persecuting the believers in Jerusalem...

Saul got what he wanted and set off in hot pursuit.

Just as Saul was nearing the city of Damascus a light from the sky flashed around him and as he fell to the ground a voice spoke to him...

Saul's travelling companions heard Jesus speak but didn't see anything.

The dazzling experience had left him completely blind so he had to be led by the hand to all the way to Damascus.

The Bible says that not only couldn't Saul see for three whole days but he also didn't eat a thing.

He was probably too shocked by the whole experience.

Meanwhile...

Across town, a man called Ananias (no, not the one who'd been killed by God for lying!) was just going about minding his own business when he had a vision (which is sort of like a dream except you can remember it when you wake up).

Boring Bible Bit Of Info: A Gentile is anybody who isn't a Jew!

Being an obedient sort of chap, Ananias did exactly as God had told him.

As he placed his hands on Saul and prayed for him, something like fish scales fell frrom his eyes and Saul's sight returned.

Saul became a follower of Jesus and was baptised and filled with the Holy Spirit.

What a turn up for the books, eh?

Just wait until the other Jews find out about this.

I'll bet they'll follow Saul's example and become believers as well.

When the Jews in Damascus realised what Saul had done they were so furious they hatched a plot to kill *him*.

They stood guard at all of the city gates and waited to catch Saul.

Saul only escaped their clutches by being lowered down the outside of the city wall in a basket at night.

That's what soldiers sometimes call out when someone approaches at night.

They want to be sure that it's not the enemy approaching before they let down their guard.

Can you imagine what the believers back in Jerusalem must have thought when they heard that *their* great enemy, Saul, was coming to pay them a visit?

They must have been scared silly!

How could they be *sure* that he'd now become a believer?

What if he was just pretending so he could trap them?

The Bible says that they took quite a bit of convincing before they let *their* guard down and allowed him to stay with them.

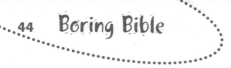

As it was, poor Saul didn't stay for long in Jerusalem.
Another bunch of Jews didn't like what he had to say about Jesus and also plotted to kill him.
Without delay, Saul was packed off to Tarsus (his home town).

While Saul's out of the way for a bit, let's check up on our old friend, fearless Peter and see what *he's* been up to...

Dear Diary

Today I travelled to Lydda to visit the believers there.
I met a paralysed man who'd been stuck in bed for eight years,
would you believe? I told him "Aeneas, Jesus Christ makes you well.
Get up and make your bed." And he did! Everyone who saw it
turned to the Lord. Between you and me I think he got off pretty
lightly. My wife nags me if I don't make my bed for just one day.
But eight years?!!!

Dear Diary

Today I went up the road to Joppa. A kind lady called Tabitha had
died and her friends begged me to hurry to her house. When I got
there they took me to the room where Tabitha was laid out and I
spent the next few minutes being given a guided tour of just about
every shirt or coat that she had made while she was alive. You'd
have thought that a roomful of weeping and wailing women was
enough to wake the dead, but obviously not. I cleared them out of
the room and then prayed to God.
"Tabitha, get up," was all I said. Then she opened her eyes and sat
up, praise to God. News spread fast and many more people came to
believe in Jesus. What a day!

Dear Diary

It has been quite an eventful few days to say the least.
There I was in Joppa, praying up on the roof in the heat of the
midday sun, just starting to feel peckish, when I had the strangest
of visions. I saw heaven open and a large sheet being lowered down
full of all kinds of animals which, as a Jew by birth, I wouldn't ever
dream of eating. Then God said to me as clear as anything "Get up,
Peter, kill and eat."

Well, did I protest or what?! I'm not going to eat food that the Jewish religion says is unclean, no way! Then God told me off and said that I shouldn't call anything unclean that he has declared clean. This happened three times just to rub it in.

While I was trying to work out what on earth it was all about, there was a knock at the door. Three men wanted me to go with them to the house of their master, Cornelius. He was a Roman Captain who loved God, and had also had a vision, but his one was starring yours truly and not a sheetful of animals! An angel from God said that he had to send for me. Well, the long and short of it was that I went with the men to Cornelius's house. God had planned it all to show me that no longer did he regard the Gentiles as unclean. The good news about Jesus was for absolutely anyone and everyone. Loads of people became believers and got baptised because of it.

Dear Diary

Sadly, John's brother James has been put to death by King Herod. Herod's always trying to suck up to the Jews. He even had me locked up and I suppose that if God hadn't intervened then I'd be dead by now as well. What happened was weird. There I was alseep in the jail, all chained up between two guards. Suddenly an angel from God woke me up. To be honest I still thought I was dreaming but I went along with it anyway. As I stood up my chains fell to the floor. The angel led me out past the first guard post and then past the second and then out into the city. Then the angel left me. I rushed to the home of some of the believers who were earnestly praying for my release. They could hardly believe their eyes when I turned up. Next day, Herod was so mad he had the guards put to death.

Boring Bible Fact: Herod himself came to a rather nasty end because he allowed the people to proclaim him to be a god. The Bible says that he was eaten by worms and died. Yuk!

Okay, back to Saul before it puts you off your food for the rest of the day!

A quick flick through the New Testament bit of the Bible will tell you that Saul was a very busy boy indeed.

Most of the rest of Acts is about *him* and *that's* not the end of it.

But first things first, Saul's going to have a name change...

HOW ABOUT **ROGER**? I CAN SEE MYSELF AS A ROGER...OR HOW ABOUT **ERIC?** YEAH, THAT SOUNDS OK! **ERIC OF *TARSUS!***

...to **Paul**. The Bible doesn't give you any clues as to *why* he

changed his name but that's what we're going to call him from now on.

As we said, Paul had been staying out of harm's way in Tarsus but now it was time to move on.

A believer called Barnabas went off to track Paul down and when he found him they both travelled to Antioch to encourage the church there for a bit.

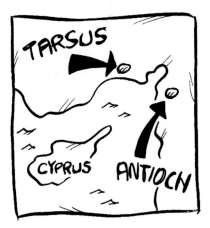

Fascinating Fact:

It was in Antioch that followers of Jesus were first called 'Christians'! It was actually meant to be a sort of nickname that their enemies used against them.

At long last, the time had come for Paul to set out to tell the world about Jesus. Many adventures lay ahead of him and as the church leaders at Antioch prayed for him and Barnabas I'm sure he must have wondered what exactly God had in store for him.

Boring Bible Joke: Did you know that the Bible records the first ever foul in the history of football?
It says that the church leaders at Antioch placed their hands on Paul and Barnabas and then SENT THEM OFF!

I'll bet you've got a favourite pop group, haven't you?
Well, any pop group that wants to gets itself well-known has got to go on tour.
But to guarantee that as many people hear you as possible then a *world* tour is an absolute *must*!
Paul wanted to make sure as many people heard about Jesus as possible so, like all good pop stars, he also went on the road.

PAUL'S AMAZING WORLD TOUR
- PART ONE -

Just before we set off, let me give you a bit of an idea of some of the places we're headed.

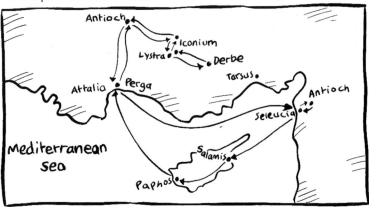

If you've got to feed the cat or put out your rubbish then do it now...we're not going to be back for a year and a half!

Okay, fasten your seatbelts.

First stop, **Cyprus**.

In Cyprus Paul wasted no time in getting himself known. Almost straight away he had a head to head with a magician called Elymas who was trying to prevent the island's governor, Sergius Paulus, from hearing about Jesus.

YOU SON OF THE DEVIL! YOU ARE THE ENEMY OF EVERYTHING THAT IS GOOD. YOU ARE FULL OF ALL KINDS OF EVIL TRICKS AND YOU ALWAYS TRY TO TURN THE LORD'S TRUTHS INTO LIES. THE LORD'S HAND WILL COME DOWN ON YOU. YOU WILL BE BLIND AND WILL NOT SEE THE LIGHT OF DAY FOR A TIME!

And blow me down, that's exactly what happened.

Elymas was struck blind and the governor became a follower of Jesus (or Christian as they were now called).

Back on the mainland Paul and Barnabas had a mixed reception as they took centre stage to tell the locals about Jesus.
Although loads of people became Christians they still got kicked out in one place and narrowly avoided getting stoned to death in another.

Lystra was a completely different kettle of fish.

In Lystra Paul and Barnabas got given the full pop star treatment when Paul healed a man who'd been lame from birth.

Paul and Barnabas were horrified and tried to put the Lystrans straight by telling them that *Jesus* did it...but it only seemed to make matters worse.

Change of plan. Instead of thinking Paul and Barnabas were the best thing since sliced bread they decided, instead, to stone them.

Paul was left for dead, laying in a heap on the ground.

Miraculously, Paul was restored after being prayed for by the believers.

Time to hit the road and make tracks for home.

Eighteen months after setting out, Paul and Barnabas were back in Antioch for a well-earned rest.

All in all, their first World Tour had been a big hit.

Things could only get better!

Getting Around In The First Century

As you can well imagine, travel in the first century wasn't plain sailing (or even plain walking for that matter).

There weren't cars, buses, aeroplanes or trains to speed people around.

A journey of a hundred miles, which by car might take you an hour and a half on a motorway, could well take you the best part of a week on foot.

If you wanted to get from A to B (or from C to D for that matter), then you didn't have too many choices.

You could either...

a Walk

b Take a chariot or horse-drawn cart

c Get a lift in a litter
(a bit like a sedan chair)

d Take a boat

e Ride on the back of an animal (but make sure you stick to things like horses and donkeys - alligators and porcupines make for an uncomfortable journey).

As for Paul and his companions, well, they probably went for the walking and sailing options most of the time so travelling around would have been jolly hard work.

Not as hard as it might have been if the Romans hadn't been busy little bees building their nice straight roads all over the place.

The Romans were famous for their roads.

Up until the Romans came on the scene, paved roads were few and far between. A road was usually just a rutted dirt track...if you were lucky!

But with their colonies spreading out for hundreds of miles in nearly every direction they needed some way of linking them all up.

Fascinating Fact:

That's where the expression comes from that 'All roads lead to Rome'. Just about every proper road really did!

Roman roads were so well made that some of them still survive to this day.

HOW TO BUILD A ROMAN ROAD

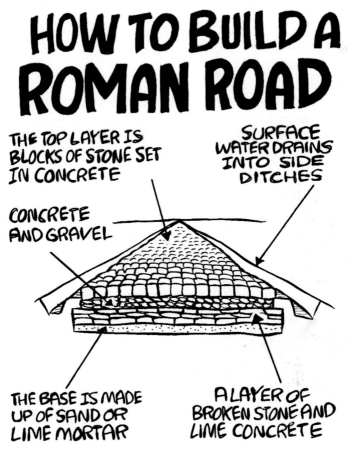

THE TOP LAYER IS BLOCKS OF STONE SET IN CONCRETE

SURFACE WATER DRAINS INTO SIDE DITCHES

CONCRETE AND GRAVEL

THE BASE IS MADE UP OF SAND OR LIME MORTAR

A LAYER OF BROKEN STONE AND LIME CONCRETE

Did You Know...?
The Romans built more than 50,000 miles of roads (80,000km)...but no service stations!

If on the other hand you needed to travel by sea then you had to pick your moment carefully, especially in the Mediterranean where most of the action in our story takes place.

The only time you could usually guarantee a safe voyage would be during the summer. The rest of the year you sailed at your peril.

Anyway, back to the story...

Mega Bust-up!

Things weren't going too well with Paul and Barnabas.
As they were getting ready to pack their bags for the second leg of their World Tour they had a bit of a sharp disagreement and fell out over whether or not they should take with them a guy called John Mark.
Barnabas said...

But Paul said...

And so, Paul and Barnabas went their separate ways.
Barnabas went off with John Mark and Paul signed up a couple
of new faces for his next tour...

PAUL'S AMAZING WORLD TOUR
- PART TWO -

Hot on the heels of his successful first tour, Paul is thinking even bigger second time around. (Well, actually, to tell the truth, he had very little idea how long this next tour was really going to take.) Paul's battle plan was simply to go back and do more of the same in the places he'd already been to.

But, as we'll soon find out, God had other ideas!

This second tour was going to take *twice* as long (that's three years) and cover nearly **3,000** miles.

All along the way, Paul strengthened and encouraged the churches.

When they got to Troas at the furthest tip of the country they got ready to enter Asia but the Holy Spirit wouldn't let them go there. He obviously had other plans.

That night, Paul had a dream.

Change of plan.

Paul's Amazing World Tour is going sailing.

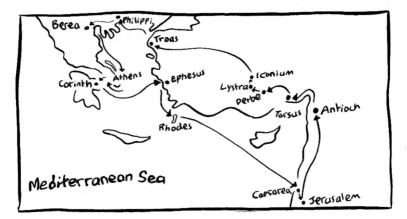

Boring Bible Fact: It was at Troas that Luke, the author of Acts, joined the group.

Once in Macedonia (that's northern Greece to you and me), they headed inland to the Roman colony of Philippi.
Whenever Paul came to a new town he nearly always made a beeline for the local synagogue so he could tell the Jews about Jesus the Messiah first.
Philippi didn't seem to have a synagogue which is why Paul went down to the river side (it was a popular place for praying), and started to talk to a group of women about Jesus. Some of them believed what Paul was saying and got baptised.

One day, as Paul and his friends were going to the place of prayer a slave-girl began to harass them...

The girl had an evil spirit inside her which was making her say these things.
It also gave her the ability to tell people's fortunes...which made a fortune for her owners.

Day in, day out, the girl would not let Paul alone and it was
beginning to get on his nerves.
Finally, Paul had had enough...

The evil spirit had no choice but to do what Paul said but the
girl's owners were none too happy.
Bang went their business before their very eyes.

They were so angry that they had Paul and Silas brought before the Roman officials who then had them flogged and beaten and thrown into jail.

How would *you* feel if you'd just been stripped, severely flogged and then been chained up by your feet in a Roman prison?

Well, the chances are you probably wouldn't be whooping it up, that's for sure.

Am I right or am I right?

But, according to the Bible, Paul and Silas passed the night singing hymns to God!!!

(If that's what they're like on a bad day, what on earth are they like on a *good* day?)

Suddenly, at around midnight, a violent earthquake shook the prison to its foundations.

All the doors flew open and the prisoners' chains fell off.

The jailer rushed to see what all the commotion was but when he saw the doors open he thought that all the prisoners had escaped.

He'd be put to death for that.

He was just pulling his sword out to kill himself, to save his Roman masters the effort, when Paul shouted at him to stop.

Phew! What a relief! The prisoners hadn't escaped after all.

The trembling jailer realised that something out of the ordinary had happened in his jail that night and Paul was able to lead the jailer and his whole household into God's Kingdom. (That's just another way of saying they all became Christians.)

The next day the Roman authorities decided to let Paul and Silas go but Paul suddenly put a spanner in the works and just about scared the pants off the Roman police officers...

To punish a Roman citizen without a proper trial was illegal and when the authorities realised what they'd done they bent over backwards to tell Paul and Silas how sorry they were.

With their grovelling done, they then asked Paul and Silas (as politely as possible) to leave the city asap (as *quickly* as possible).

Everywhere Paul went, trouble seemed to followed him.

As Paul's World Tour rolled relentlessly on it was the same in just about every town and city he stopped off at...

THESSALONICA GAZETTE

RIOTS IN CITY

Jealous Jews today attacked the home of Jason, who was playing host to Paul and Silas, the infamous Christians who are presently touring the region with their new brand of religion.

CORINTH CHRONICLE

BEATEN-UP IN COURT!

Jealous Jews vented their anger on Sosthenes the synagogue leader, after trying unsuccessfully to get Paul, the Christian convicted of breaking their laws Gallio, the Roman governor of Achaia didn't bat an eyelid as Sosthenes was badly beaten right in front of him.

The Bible says that Paul stayed in Corinth for a year and a half, preaching and teaching about Jesus.

Eventually, Paul and his companions made their way back to Antioch by way of Jerusalem.

Boring Bible Fact: Did you know that Paul was a tentmaker by trade. Whenever he was short of cash he would turn his hand to making the odd tent or two!

Believe It Or Not...!

Paul travelled all over the vast Roman Empire telling people about Jesus and on the way he met people who worshipped all kinds of different gods or had lots of weird and wonderful ideas and beliefs about life.

One of the things that interested people then as much as it does today was astrology and fortune telling.

Another thing that Paul saw a lot of was people meddling with magic powers to make things happen. (Read Boring Bible book *Magnificent Moses* and you'll find out just what God thought about that sort of stuff!)

Anyway, just so you know what Paul was up against as he went from town to town, here's a small selection of some of the gods that people worshipped.

For starters there were the gods of the Greeks...

Baal - she was a goddess who was thought to influence the seasons - so if you wanted a good harvest then she was who you made offerings to.

Zeus - he was a Greek god who was supposed to be the big cheese (the bossman in charge of all the other gods). He was also reputed to be a right nasty piece of work.

Greek religion was the centre of city life with massive festivals for all the family to take part in.

Even the Olympic Games were first held in honour of the god Zeus.

Unfortunately, these gods still didn't make them happy or give the people who worshipped them any answers about life, death and the universe.

On top of all those gods, there were the **philosophers** who tried to work out everything in their minds with lots of clever ideas about the world and life.

When it came to religion, the Romans were a bit unimaginative (they were probably far too busy planning new conquests and building roads to bother about such trivial things), so they simply took over many of the Greek gods and gave them new names such as Zeus who became Jupiter.

Some of the Romans' hot favourite gods were...

Mars - he was the god of war
Apollo - he was the god of wisdom
Artemis - that was Apollo's twin sister (look out for her on Paul's next tour!)
Aphrodite - the goddess of love.

As to what Romans believed, not a lot is known.
Basically, they thought that some great power ruled nature so they created gods for just about anything and everything including gods of the house and gods of the fields.

All in all, living in the Roman Empire meant that you could believe just about whatever you wanted to.
Now here's *your* chance to let your imagination run riot.
Just for a bit of fun, make up the whackiest things you can think of that the Romans might have believed, like...

Boiled eggs need to be treated with a bit more respect, (no more bashing them with a spoon or slicing their tops off with a knife), or else the gods will be angry with you.

Or (over to you)...

....
....
....
....
....
....

....
....
....
....
....
....
....
....
....
....
....
....
....

Crazy isn't it?

If everyone believed whatever they liked then none of their beliefs were really worth a jot, were they?

That didn't seem to bother the Romans in the slightest.

To be quite honest, what they believed had little or no effect on how they lived anyway.

What *really* counted was...**being a good Roman citizen**!

PAUL'S AMAZING WORLD TOUR
- PART THREE -

I'm afraid it's time once again to pack your bags.

We're not sticking around in Antioch for long.

There are now thousands and thousands of Christians out there who are itching to see Paul again.

Not only that but there are still loads more who haven't even heard of him or, for that matter, the good news about Jesus.

This tour is going to be the tour to beat all tours...

TICKET

PAUL'S 3rd WORLDWIDE TOUR
- Four years duration -
- 2,700 miles (roughly!)

Just in case you want to look at a pretty map to show you what places Paul's Tour is headed, here's another map...

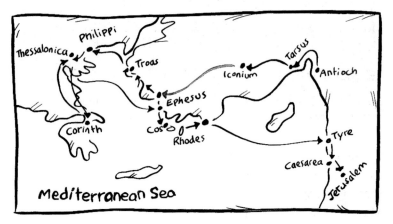

After doing some really good stuff along the way, Paul ended up in a place called Ephesus.

Little did Paul know it, but he was going to be here for the next three years.

Such was Paul's success in Ephesus that things finally came to a head...

Which they reluctantly did.
Phew! That was a close shave!
In time, Paul and his trusty band set off on tour again.
After doing a nice little roundabout visit to some of the cities bordering the Aegean Sea they were back in Troas.

ZZZZZZZZZZZ!

If you're anything like me, you can only sit and listen to somebody talking for so long before your eyelids start to feel heavy and all you want to do is sleep.

One Saturday night, Paul was out for a meal...

Er, not quite.
More like...

Next day, Paul would be moving on, so he didn't want to miss
an opportunity to speak about Jesus.
All through the meal and through the evening Paul talked.
And talked.
And talked.
He kept *on* talking about Jesus...and *on* and *on* and *on* and *on*!
By midnight, some of the dinner guests were beginning to feel a
bit sleepy.

Perish the thought!

The Bible says that a young man called Eutychus was sitting by the window.

As the evening turned to night, Eutychus got sleepier and sleepier until...

They were three storeys up and the fall killed the young man. Paul raced downstairs, threw himself on the lad, hugged him and...Eutychus came back to life.

What a miracle!

And I thought that young people were meant to be able to stay up all night *without* getting tired!!!

Eventually, Paul said his farewells to the people of Ephesus and set off back to Jerusalem.

Just before he reached Israel's capital city, Paul popped in to see some of the Christians in Caesarea. While he was there he bumped into (not literally!) a prophet called Agabus.
Agabus took hold of Paul's belt, tied him up, hand and foot and said...

How strange!
All the believers begged Paul not to go to Jerusalem but Paul said he was prepared not only to be tied up in Jerusalem but to die for Jesus if needs be.

Now, what I want *you* to do (yes, you, the reader!), is make a mental note of what Agabus said to Paul so we can find out whether he was telling the truth or not.

But first...

A Who's Who Of The Roman Emperors

When it boiled down to it, the whole Roman world revolved around the emperor.
He was the main man in Rome and what he said went.
The New Testament bit of the Bible mentions quite a few

different emperors so it can sometimes be a bit confusing who was in charge when.

So here's a run down of who was calling the shots in the Roman Empire...

Augustus - he ruled from 30 BC to AD 14 so he was emperor when Jesus Christ was born.

Tiberius - he ruled from AD 14 to AD 37 so he was emperor at the time of Jesus's death.

Caligula - he ruled from AD 37 to AD 41 but doesn't get a mention in the Bible.

Claudius - he was Caligula's uncle and was responsible for chucking all the Jews out of Rome. He was on the throne from AD 41 to AD 54 but he came to a rather gruesome end. His wife, Agrippina (who was also his niece!), fed him poison mushrooms which killed him. This made way for her thirteen-year-old son by another marriage to become the next emperor. His name was...

Nero - his ruthless rule lasted from AD 54 to AD 68 and he took a leaf out of his mother's book and also murdered a close member of the family. In fact, it was his *mother* he murdered!

Nero had a bit of a reputation for being violent and even kicked one of his wives to death!

His behaviour even shocked the usually unshockable Romans.

To top it all off he then set about persecuting and torturing the Christians to distract people's attention from his disastrous rule.

Nero held the reins of the Roman Empire for the whole of the time that Paul was travelling around.

For those first-century Christians, Roman rule had its good side and its bad side. On the one hand...

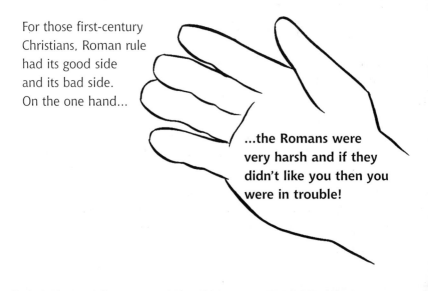

...the Romans were very harsh and if they didn't like you then you were in trouble!

On the other hand...

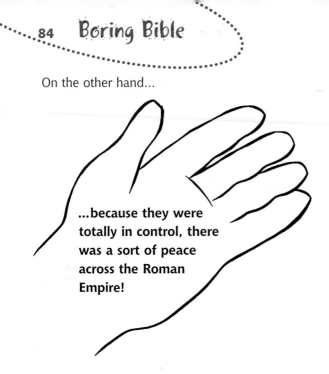

...because they were totally in control, there was a sort of peace across the Roman Empire!

The Romans called this peace PAX ROMANA which is simply Latin for ROMAN PEACE. Pax Romana made it safe and easy for Paul and his companions to travel and spread the gospel without fear of attack.

(Not forgetting, of course, those handy new Romans roads, without which *none* of it would have been possible.)

It's All Greek To Me!

Another good thing about the Roman Empire was that just about everyone spoke the same language.

Although the Romans had Latin and the Jews had Aramaic, the language that people used in day to day conversation was *Greek*.

Just like the United States owes many things like language,
religion, law and literature to Great Britain, so the Roman
Empire had the Greeks to thank for their culture and way of life.

Now, I think it's about time we were getting back to Paul...

"You're Nicked, Paul!"

Agabus had been wasting his breath when he warned Paul
about going into Jerusalem. Paul completely ignored him and
entered the great city.

Look out, look out, trouble's about!

It didn't take long for the Jews to start stirring things up.

They mistakenly thought that Paul had taken some Gentiles into
the Temple (which was a big no-no), and because of that they
caused a near riot.

Paul was dragged out of the Temple by the angry mob but was rescued by the Roman commander and his troops just in the nick of time.

When the Roman commander realised that Paul *wasn't* a troublemaker he allowed him to speak to the crowd.
Paul gave them a potted version of his life story to try and convince them that Jesus really was the Messiah that the Jews had been promised by God.
Their response was predictable.
They weren't buying it!

The Bible says that the Romans then took Paul away to have him whipped to find out why the Jews were screaming blue murder.

(You'd have thought they could have just *asked* him, wouldn't you?)

Ooer!

That put the wind up the Roman commander.

The Romans took their laws extremely seriously and he would have been in big trouble with his superiors if he'd mistreated another Roman citizen such as Paul without a proper trial.

In an attempt to get to the bottom of the Jews' complaints the commander decided on another plan of action...

THE ROMAN COMMANDER CORDIALLY INVITES

The entire Jewish Council and Chief Priests

TO MAKE PLAIN THEIR ACCUSATIONS AGAINST PAUL, TOMORROW

R.S.V.P.

Be there or _be_ square!

So, the very next day, Paul was up before the Jewish Council to defend himself.

The Jews were so angry at Paul that one of those standing close by took a swipe at him as he started to speak but Paul then went and put the cat among the pigeons when he started to talk about whether or not there was life after death.

Harmless enough, you might think, but you'd be wrong. The Pharisees (they were a Jewish religious group) believed _one_ thing but the Sadducees (another Jewish religious group) believed _another_ thing.

Both groups completely forgot about Paul for a bit and started squabbling with each other. Clever tactic, Paul!

I DON'T LIKE SQUABBLING! THAT'S WHY I'M SAD, YOU SEE!

Then they remembered about Paul again, so, for his own safety he was whisked away to the Roman fort.

That night Paul was visited by God himself.

Those Jews Just Don't Give Up!

The next morning, over 40 Jews made a vow not to eat or drink anything until they had killed Paul.

When news of this reached the Roman commander's ears he sprung into action.

With an armed guard of 200 soldiers, 200 spearman and 70 horsemen (seems a wee bit excessive to me but I'm sure they know best), Paul was taken to Caesarea to the safekeeping of the governor Felix.

Five days later, guess who turned up in Caesarea?

Yes, you're right, it was the Jews.

(I'll bet those 40 vowing Jews were getting pretty peckish by now.)

Together with a grovelling lawyer called Tertullus, they tried once again to press charges against Paul.

Felix couldn't quite make up his mind what to do so he decided to keep Paul where he was for a bit.

The 'bit' lasted two years until Felix was replaced by Festus.
Festus wanted to please the Jews so he just kept Paul locked up.
The Jews begged Festus to bring Paul back to Jerusalem, and he
probably would have done if Paul hadn't done what all Roman
citizens could do as a last resort...

That meant that Paul would now have to go to Rome and plead
his case before the most powerful man on the face of the earth.

Festus had no alternative but to agree to Paul's request.

Boring Bible Fact: Once again, Luke, the writer of Acts, accompanied Paul all the way to Rome. We know this because it keeps talking about 'we' did this and 'we' did that!

Voyage Of Destruction

The quickest way to get to Rome (unless you were a bird) was by ship but even then it was a journey of about 2,500 miles which is not much fun if you get seasick!

Just like the United States and most other nations, Great Britain has a national anthem.

The national anthem of Great Britain has the lines...

RULE BRITANNIA, BRITANNIA RULES THE WAVES...

...and so on and so on.

But if you happened to be alive at the same time as Paul then it wasn't the British that ruled the waves...it was the **Romans**! Not content with conquering the land, they'd also conquered the sea.

To be precise, the *Mediterranean* Sea.

The Mediterranean was busy with ships sailing to and fro, taking cargoes to the farthest corners of the Roman Empire. The Egyptians, for their part, exported vast quantities of grain by sea all the way up to Italy.

The ships were as much as 200 feet long (that's 60 metres), and were carried straight across to their destination by the strong summer winds.

Winter and spring, the corn ships sailed in shorter hops, keeping close to the land for fear of being blown off course in the terrible storms.

It was this sort of corn ship that Paul was put on to.

With a Roman officer called Julius in charge, Paul and a whole bunch of other prisoners set sail.

The first part of the voyage was plain sailing (literally), as the ship sailed close to shore.

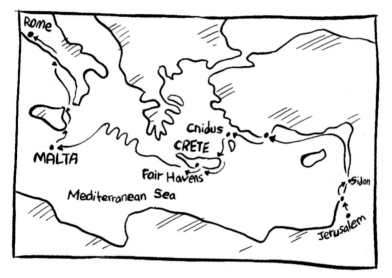

By the time they reached Crete, October was just about on them and the safe-sailing season had well and truly passed.

The ship anchored in a place called Fair Havens but both the captain and the owner of the ship wanted to find a better harbour to spend the winter.

Paul felt uneasy about heading out to sea once again.

He warned them that continuing the voyage would be very dangerous and very unwise.

Ignoring Paul's advice they set sail but what they hadn't bargained on was the ferocious wind that suddenly blew up as they edged round the coast of Crete.

It carried them out into the open sea and for many days everyone (except for Paul) lived in fear of their lives.

The storm was so bad they couldn't tell whether it was night or day, such was the darkness.

For two terrifying weeks they were tossed and blown across the Mediterranean Sea.

At the end of two weeks they realised that they were at last nearing land...

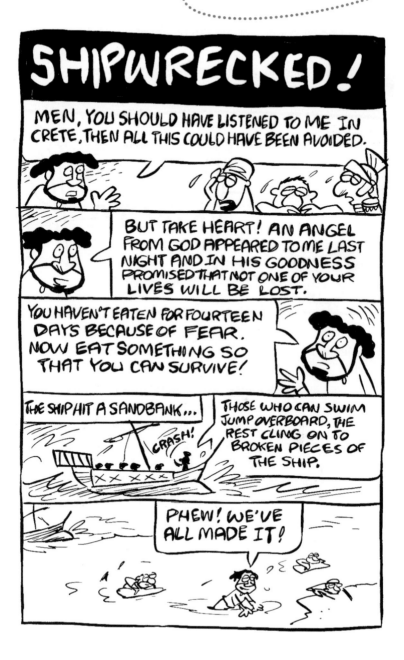

Just as God had promised, all **276** on board survived.

It didn't take them long to find out the name of the island that they'd run aground on...

The Mediterranean islands aren't all hot sunshine and sandy beaches.
When Paul and his shipmates came ashore it was tipping it down with rain and not only only that it was also rather nippy.
Fortunately for them the Maltese were a friendly bunch and lit a fire and made them feel at home.
It's amazing to think that one itty bitty little fire could be responsible for what happened next...

MALTA MAIL

SNAKE BITE MAN LIVES!

The survivor of a shipwreck off the coast of Malta was warming himself around a fire when a snake, driven out by the heat, bit his hand. The man, called Paul, suffered no ill-effects at all, not even any swelling. After a long wait, the man was still very much alive, so the conclusion was reached that he must be a god, a charge that Paul hotly denies.

Paul siezed the opportunity his fame brought and for the next three months went around telling the Maltese people about Jesus and healing their sick.

From Malta, Paul was taken to Rome where he continued to tell both Jews and Gentiles alike all about Jesus.
For two years Paul was under house arrest, which meant he could still see his friends and have visitors. But there, in Rome, Paul's story abruptly ends as told in the book of Acts.

Boring Bible Info: From what we know, Paul did probably have the chance to go before Caesar in Rome. He was then thought to have been released and might well have even preached in Spain. It is thought that Paul was finally executed by Nero in about AD 67.

What an extraordinary man Paul was.
He had achieved what he had set out to do...to take the good news of Jesus to Europe!

Fascinating Fact:

The book of Acts mentions more than 30 countries, 50 towns or cities, loads and loads of islands, and nearly 100 people!

Dear Sir...

Nowadays, if you want to contact a friend there are a number of choices open to you.

You can either...
1 E-mail them
2 Text them
3 Phone them
4 Fax them
5 Write to them.

There might be other ways that you can think of but these are the most popular.
When Paul and the other believers were alive nearly 2000 years ago they didn't have computers or phones so their choices were much more limited.
If you had something to say then it was a jolly old letter or nothing!

HOW TO WRITE A LETTER
IN THE
FIRST CENTURY A.D.

FIRST OFF, YOU'RE GOING TO NEED TO GET YOUR HANDS ON SOME **PAPYRUS**. (THAT'S WHAT YOU'RE GOING TO WRITE ON!) IF YOUR LOCAL STORE IS FRESH OUT OF PAPYRUS THEN WHY NOT HAVE A GO AT MAKING SOME YOURSELF!
YOU'LL NEED TO CUT DOWN SOME PAPYRUS PLANTS AND SLICE UP THE TRIANGULAR-SHAPED STEMS INTO THIN STRIPS...

...HAMMER THEM FLAT...

...THEN PASTE THE PIECES INTO A ROLL...

...NOW TAKE A HOLLOW REED STALK AND SHARPEN ONE OF THE ENDS TO A POINT AND THERE YOU HAVE YOUR VERY OWN FIRST-CENTURY PEN!
DIP THE PEN INTO SOME INK AND AWAY YOU GO!

Boring Bible Fact: The early Christians could be partly responsible for making books with pages so popular. Around the second century they started to produce the Bible in pages, (which were a lot easier to handle), rather than long scrolls.

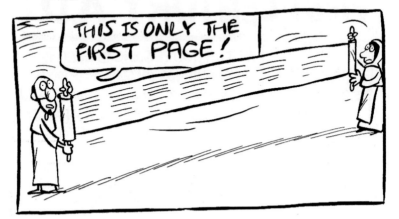

I'll bet you're wondering why I've told you all this info, aren't you?

The answer's simple.

It's because Paul (and some of the other early Christians) wrote heaps and heaps of letters. They're all reprinted in the Bible for us to have a peek at.

In fact, just about a whole *third* of the New Testament bit of the Bible is made up of letters!

How would you feel if *your* letters got made public?

Actually, Paul and the others didn't mind their letters being read one little bit.

The stuff that they put in them was meant to encourage all the different churches that they had already visited on their World Tour.

What they wrote is still very useful to Christians in the modern world.

Some of the letters Paul wrote were even written while he was chained up in prison but that didn't stop him.

Are you interested in finding out about some of the things that Paul and Co. wrote?

Okay, let's take a quick peek at some snippets...

Dear Church in Rome

Sin came into the world through one man, Adam, which brought with it death. But think how much more was done by one man, Jesus Christ! Everyone who receives God's goodness can be put right again. So, once you've made Jesus Christ your master, don't keep on sinning! The Holy Spirit living inside you will make sure you know that you are God's children, so don't keep trying to please yourselves. Instead, do your best to please God. After all, God is the one who's on your side!
Keep up the good work.

Love

Paul

✝

Dear Church in Corinth

Don't start thinking that anyone of you is more important than the others. Jesus's church is like his <u>body</u> to do his work. How daft for an eye to think that the rest of the body doesn't <u>need</u> it or the foot to think that the hand is needed more. <u>Rubbish!!!</u> One can't do without the other, so look after each other and you'll get along a lot better! which reminds me...
Using all the amazing spiritual gifts God has given you is great but if you don't have any love for each other then you <u>might</u> <u>as well</u> <u>forget</u> it!

love

Paul

Dear Church in Ephesus

First off, all you wives out there, you need to make sure you respect your husbands. But it doesn't end there because husbands, you need to make even _Surer_ that you love your wives just like Jesus Christ loves his church. And a word to you kids! Do what your parents tell you, if you want a good, long life.' On the other hand, parents, don't treat your kids badly. Tell them about Jesus and train them up properly. And all of you, a word to the wise. _Watch out for the devil_. He's out to get you. Don't start getting jittery. As long as you stick close to God and keep your guard up, you've got _nothing to fear!_

Love

Paul

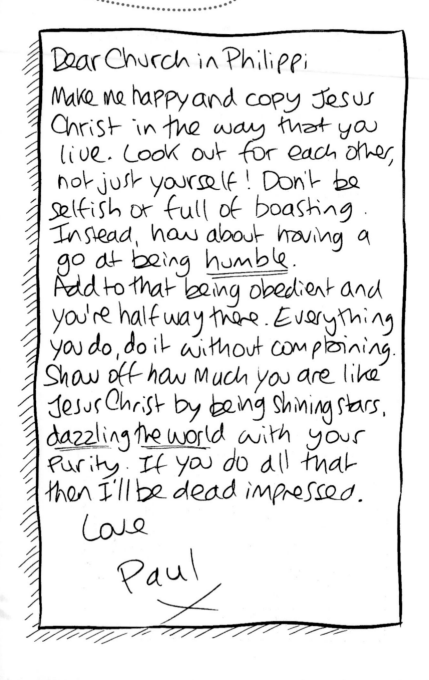

Dear Church in Philippi

Make me happy and copy Jesus Christ in the way that you live. Look out for each other, not just yourself! Don't be selfish or full of boasting. Instead, how about having a go at being <u>humble</u>.
Add to that being obedient and you're half way there. Everything you do, do it without complaining. Show off how much you are like Jesus Christ by being shining stars, <u>dazzling the world</u> with your purity. If you do all that then I'll be dead impressed.

Love

Paul

A Quick Guide To What Happened When

AD 37 Paul becomes a Christian

AD 47 - 49 Paul's World Tour - Part One

AD 51 - 53 Paul's World Tour - Part Two

AD 54 - 57 Paul's World Tour - Part Three

AD 58 Paul arrested in Jerusalem

AD 60 Paul appeals to Caesar

AD 61 - 62 Paul's two-year house arrest.

AD 67 Paul executed

AD 70 Jerusalem destroyed.

So, that just about wraps it up for the New Testament.
We've seen how the Holy Spirit got the church up and running
soon after Jesus had gone back into heaven and then we saw
how it exploded all over Europe.

What next?
Is that where the Bible leaves it?
Is that the end of the story?
Does God have anything else up his sleeve?
Well, surprise, surprise, the Bible doesn't leave us guessing.
But, first, I've got a bit of bad news.

If you've read Boring Bible book *Super Son* as well as reading this book then it will be pretty obvious what most people thought about Jesus. As far as *they* were concerned there was absolutely no way that he was the Messiah they had been told by God to expect.

The Bible says that many times Jesus warned them *not* to reject him or God would punish them by sending an enemy army to attack and destroy them.

The Jewish people didn't heed Jesus's advice.
Most of them would have nothing to do with Jesus and even worse than that some of them reckoned he was working for the devil himself.

Payback Time

In AD 66, according to a Jewish historian called Josephus, the Roman General, Cestius, marched on Israel's capital city, Jerusalem.

The Jews fought so furiously that the Romans decided to retreat back to Caesarea.

According to Josephus...

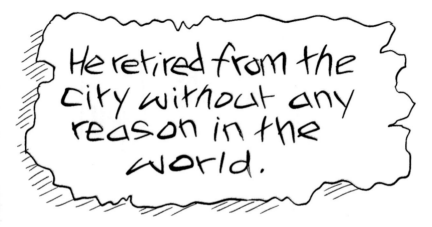

He retired from the city without any reason in the world.

Or was there a reason?

It would seem that God was giving the *Christians* a chance to escape.

Take a look at what Jesus said when he was warning about the attack on Jersualem...

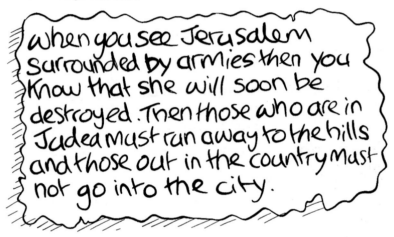

When you see Jerusalem surrounded by armies then you know that she will soon be destroyed. Then those who are in Judea must run away to the hills and those out in the country must not go into the city.

Remembering what Jesus had said, thousands fled the city.
How do we know this?
Well, once again we've got good old Josephus to thank...

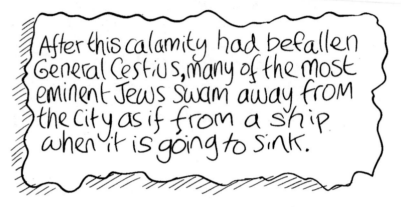

After this calamity had befallen General Cestius, many of the most eminent Jews swam away from the city as if from a ship when it is going to sink.

Boring Bible Fact: It was another historian called Hegessippus who actually tells us that those Jews were in fact Christians!

The Jews left in the city thought they'd beaten the Romans fair and square.

They hadn't banked on nasty Nero getting extremely hot under the collar.

Back came the Romans, this time with a new commander, General Vespasian and his son Titus.

The Size Of The Roman Army

Three legions (a legion is up to 6000 soldiers).

31 cohorts.

6000 archers.

Thousands of horsemen.

Which made a grand total, according to Josephus, of **60,000** (and we'll take his word for it!).

Stop grumbling, you can put your weapons down for a bit.
Those Romans won't be attacking you for a while yet.
For what reason?
Easy.
Without warning, Nero had died (how inconsiderate of him) and
Vespasian had to rush back to Rome to take over as emperor.
That left his son Titus in charge.
It was going to take a bit of time for the Romans to get
organised again so that gave the Jews a bit of a breathing space.
I wonder how they spent their time?

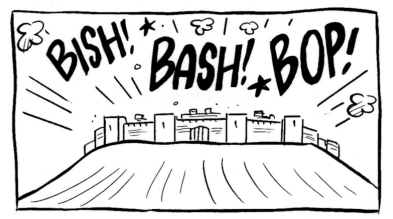

The Jews, having nothing better to do, started to fight and
bicker amongst themselves over who should be running the
show.

When at last the Roman army did eventually reach Jerusalem
many of the inhabitants had already been killed by other Jews.

Let Battle Commence

Titus's army was posted seven deep, right around the city, so that none of the three million Jews could escape.

Next, he built rows and rows of earth banks to encircle Jerusalem with three 75-foot towers for shooting missiles. (The wood for the towers was carted in from eleven miles around the city.)

The Roman army battered their way into the city destroying anybody and everything that lay in their path.

To the horror of the Jews their magnificent Temple was burnt to the ground.

Titus had said to leave it but the Roman soldiers were so full of anger that they went ahead and torched it anyway.

Except for 97,000 young men under seventeen years of age (who were led away as slaves to work in the mines of Egypt), all three million people were killed by the invading Roman army. Over a million of them were there just for the Passover celebrations.

If only they'd heeded Jesus's warnings and *not* gone back into the city then they might still have been alive.

To finish off the job, the Romans completely destroyed the entire city and then the rubble was ploughed over by oxen as if it had never existed!

Fascinating Fact:

If you go to Rome you can still see the carvings on the Arch of Titus which show the Roman army carrying away the spoils of war from Jerusalem.

Just for the record, God hadn't completely given up on the Jews. When he started their nation thousands of years earlier with a man called Abraham (check out Boring Bible book *Hotchpotch Hebrews*), God made a covenant with them (that's like a special promise) that he would *always* be their God...no matter what! The Bible even tells us that one day, thousands upon thousands of the Jewish people are going to suddenly realise that Jesus really *was* God's promised Messiah after all and become his followers.

Popeye's Girlfriend

If you're a fan of Popeye the sailor man then you'll know all

about his skinny girlfriend, Olive Oyl.

If you read the Bible, olive oil (not Popeye's girlfriend) keeps cropping up all over the place.

That's because olives were important to the people living around the Mediterranean.

The Bible says that the Jewish nation is like the branches of an olive tree (the tree is meant to represent Jesus himself)...

...but when the Jews *rejected* Jesus as their Messiah it was like they were saying that they wanted nothing to do with the olive tree.

(Which was pretty daft really considering that a branch gets all its life from the tree!)

So God chopped the Jewish branches off...

...and grafted on *Gentile* (non-Jewish) branches to replace them. But the Bible says that the Gentiles shouldn't get smug because

one day some of the original Jewish branches will be grafted back on again just like God promised.

The Grand Finale

Can you imagine how annoying it would be to see a film or read a book that didn't have a proper ending?

Well, just in case you didn't know, not only does the Bible have a beginning and a middle...but it also has an *end*.
That's a relief!

But why, you may ask, does the Bible *need* to have an end?

I said you *may* ask, I didn't say you *had* to!

Couldn't things just keep on going the way they are?
I'm afraid not!
The Bible says that one day Jesus is going to come back to earth again.
Did you know that?
If you didn't, then here are some things that the Bible tells us will happen when he does...

1 Jesus will take back control of the world (which Adam handed over to Satan).
2 Jesus will get rid of Satan once and for all (the Bible says he's going to be thrown into a terrible place called hell as his punishment).
3 Sickness and sadness will be a thing of the past.
4 There'll be no more wars.
5 There'll be no more hunger.
6 Everyone who doesn't love Jesus will be punished by not going to heaven.
7 God will make a brand new heaven and a brand new earth.
8 Everyone who loves Jesus will be with him for ever and ever.

Boring Bible Fact: There were over 300 prophecies (a bit like adverts) for Jesus in the Bible before he was born and they all came true. But, there are over *1800* references to Jesus *returning!* I guess God wants us to be absolutely clear that we really *can* expect Jesus to come back.

But, Jesus's second time around visit won't be like his first.
It won't be all shepherds, wise men and stables.
No, the Bible says that next time he'll come back like a conquering king with all the angels of heaven.
Wow! That's going be awesome!
It also says that we should be ready.

Get Ready!

If you're going on holiday then you'll probably get a few things
ready (unless of course you're really lazy).
Make a quick list of some of the things you'd take...

MY GET READY FOR HOLIDAY LIST...

Okay, now, how about making a list of the things you think
you're going to need to get ready for when Jesus returns.
(Get ready list over page.)

MY GET READY FOR JESUS LIST...

It's a bit harder isn't it?
Let me give you some suggestions...

MY GET READY FOR JESUS LIST...

1. Make sure I'm a follower of Jesus.
2. Live my life to please God.
3. Try to love other people like God/uer me.
4. Go all out for God..
5.
6.
7.

Can you think of any more?

So, that's just about it for the New Testament bit of the Bible. But the story of the Church doesn't end there...it was really just the *beginning*.

Because Jesus is very much alive, he's still changing lives 2000 years later.

It's reckoned that roughly **70,000** people every week become Christians around the world and there are thought to be about **two billion** followers of Jesus in total.

Not bad for something that started out as just 120 people crammed into a house in Jerusalem on the day of Pentecost!

The Bit At The End

Just before we say our farewells, let's take one last look at some of the stuff that we've covered in this book...

What's Been Happening?

The Holy Spirit fills Peter and the other disciples of Jesus.
The Church begins and then grows (lots of miracles).
Stephen killed for being a Christian (Paul was there!).
Paul becomes a Christian.
Paul goes travelling.
Lots of people become followers of Jesus.
Lots of people become haters of Jesus (especially Jews).
Paul goes travelling again.
Paul goes travelling again, again!
Paul gets arrested.
Jews try to kill him.
Lots of letters get written by Paul and Co.
Paul gets to tell loads of important people about Jesus (including, eventually, Caesar).
Paul gets killed.

A Reminder Of The Main Characters

Peter
Luke (the author of Acts)
Stephen (the first martyr)
Lots of Jews and Jewish religious leaders
Paul (previously known as Saul)
Barnabas (who eventually had a 'Barny' with Paul)
Silas
Timothy
Various Roman emperors
And, of course, all the people who became part of the Church in the first century AD!

Now it's *your* turn!
Write down which bits of the Bible you don't find boring any more...

Well, that just about wraps up the Bible (that's if you've read all **six Boring Bible** books). One more thing. What would *really* help you is to get your hands on a proper Bible so you can look up all the brill stuff that we didn't have space for. There are some great versions around that are just for kids.
Have fun!

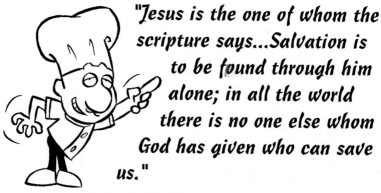

"Jesus is the one of whom the scripture says...Salvation is to be found through him alone; in all the world there is no one else whom God has given who can save us."

Acts 4: 11-12

We know that in all things God works for good with those who love him.

Romans 8: 28

,CHOMP!。

'CHEW!。

、MUNCH!。

If God is for us, who can be against us?

Romans 8: 31

God is light, and there is no darkness at all in him.

1 John 1:5

SLURP!

God is love.

1 John 4:16

Love is patient and kind; it is not jealous or conceited or proud; love is not ill-mannered or selfish or irritable; love does not keep a record of wrongs; love is not happy with evil, but is happy with the truth. Love never gives up.

1 Corinthinans 13:4-7

MUNCH!

Then I saw a new heaven and a new earth. The first heaven and the first earth disappeared, and the sea vanished. And I saw the Holy City, the new Jerusalem, coming down out of heaven from God, prepared and ready, like a bride dressed to meet her husband. I heard a loud voice speaking from the throne: 'Now God's home is with mankind! He will live with them, and they shall be his people. God himself will be with them, and he will be their God. He will wipe away all tears from their eyes. There will be no more death, no more grief or crying or pain. The old things have disappeared'.

Revelation 21:1-4

CHEW!

NIBBLE!